Learning English
book for all ages

word search game

BACK TO

SCHOOL

ALPHABET

ABCDEFGHIJKLMNOPQRSTUVWXYZ
:!#?;☐◉$½±8✳1234567890

Table of contents

Page No.

Alphabet A-Z

- A 4
- B 5
- C 6
- D 7
- E 8
- F 9
- G 10
- H 11
- I 12
- J 13
- K 14
- L 15
- M 16
- N 17
- O 18
- P 19
- Q 20
- R 21
- S 22
- T 23
- U 24
- V 25
- W 26
- Y 27
- Z 28

Path Game : Find Path and Maze Game 29-31

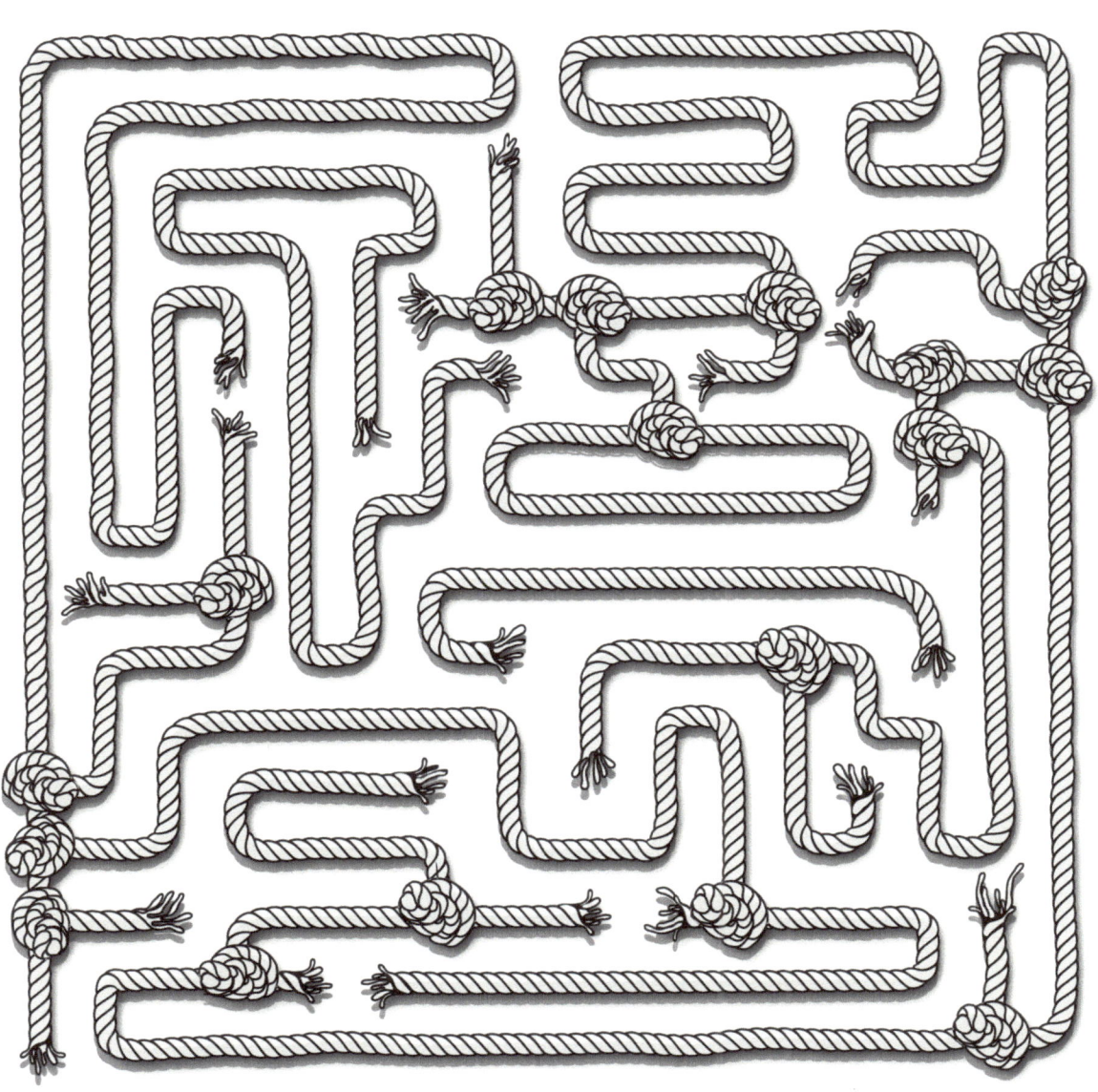

(3)

CHOSE THE CORRECT WORDS - A

African   **Alien**   **Angel**   **Airplane**

CHOSE THE CORRECT WORDS - B

Bee	Baker	Bicycle	Baby

CHOSE THE CORRECT WORDS - C

Cat	Castle	Crane	Coast-guard

CHOSE THE CORRECT WORDS - D

Dinosaur   **Dancing**   **Dragon**   **Drums**

CHOSE THE CORRECT WORDS - E

| Eyeglasses | Elephant | Elk | Evolution |

CHOSE THE CORRECT WORDS - F

Fisherman   **Frog**   **Feather**   **Ferris wheel**

CHOSE THE CORRECT WORDS - G

Globe   Graduation   Guitar   Ghost

CHOSE THE CORRECT WORDS - H

Hair clip   Hands   Horse   House

CHOSE THE CORRECT WORDS - I

Ink	Ice-skate	Ice-cream	Infinity

CHOSE THE CORRECT WORDS - J

Jar   **Jeans**   **Jug**   **Jeep**

CHOSE THE CORRECT WORDS - K

Key   **Knife**   **Kiss**   **Keyboard**

CHOSE THE CORRECT WORDS - L

| Ladder | Lion | Legs | Laptop |

CHOSE THE CORRECT WORDS - M

Monument   Mother   Mermaid   Mosquito

CHOSE THE CORRECT WORDS - N

Numbers   Notes   Ninja   Necklace

CHOSE THE CORRECT WORDS - O

Oldster　　　**Oil**　　　**Owl**　　　**Octopus**

CHOSE THE CORRECT WORDS - P

Photographer   Policeman   Puzzles   Pregnancy

CHOSE THE CORRECT WORDS - Q

CHOSE THE CORRECT WORDS - R

Rabbit   **Rose**   **Roof**   **Robber**

CHOSE THE CORRECT WORDS - S

Squirrel   **Shark**   **Stork**   **Seahorse**

CHOSE THE CORRECT WORDS - T

Teapot Tree Tyre Teeth

CHOSE THE CORRECT WORDS - U

Urban area	Umbrella	Unicorn	Universe

CHOSE THE CORRECT WORDS - V

Video cassette	Van	Violin	Video game

CHOSE THE CORRECT WORDS - W

Woman   **Wig**   **Wolf**   **Witch**

CHOSE THE CORRECT WORDS - Y

Youth   **Yam**   **Yoga**   **Yacht**

CHOSE THE CORRECT WORDS - Z

Zigzag	Zebra	Zip	Zero

Try A, B or C that a squirrel will get walnuts.

Which the right Path a Bird Will go Back home??
Let' try!!!

Which the right Path a fish will go to Coral??
Let' try!!!

Produced & Edited by

Crystal S. Christensen

In 2019.